COLORS OF

New York

AA Publishing

Author: Donna Dailey

Produced by AA Publishing

Text © Automobile Association Developments Limited 2004

Published by AA Publishing (a trading name of Automobile Association Developments Limited, whose registered office is Southwood East, Apollo Rise, Farnborough, Hampshire, GU14 0JW; registered number 1878835).

ISBN 0-7495-4240-3

A01958

A CIP catalogue record for this book is available from the British Library.

Printed and bound in China

COLORS OF

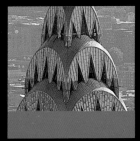

New York

CONT

ENTS

COLORS OF **NEW YORK**

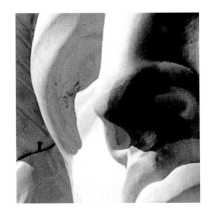

INTROD

COLORS OF NEW YORK: **INTRODUCTION**

New York is like no other city on earth. Other places may have the same elements—skyscrapers, world-class museums, cutting-edge art and theater, power houses of fashion and finance—but no place mixes them up in quite the same way. The extra ingredient that makes New York such a heady cocktail is its energy, a palpable buzz that courses through the city day and night, heightening every experience.

Although the city includes four other boroughs—Brooklyn, the Bronx, Queens, and Staten Island—Manhattan will always be its pulsating heart. Packed onto a narrow island between the Hudson and East rivers, it measures just 13.5 miles (22km) long and 2.25 miles (3.5km) wide. The Dutch settlers who purchased Manhattan from the Native Americans in 1626 for $24 worth of trinkets would be amazed to find that today their colony is sited on some of the most expensive land on the planet.

From early days
From colonial times, New York's fine harbor and its position at the confluence of the Hudson River and the Atlantic Ocean brought prosperity. It became the world's busiest port and the center of trade in the United States. It also became the gateway to America for millions of immigrants, whose first footsteps in the New World were on the shores of Lower Manhattan.

By 1900, New York had become the second largest city in the world, after London. Today, in 17th place, just behind Tokyo, New York is a city of 8 million residents. It remains a mecca for people from around the world as well as from throughout the United States. New York is the country's great melting pot.

The sum of its parts
There is no such thing as a typical New Yorker. They are street vendors, taxi drivers, police officers, writers and artists, models and moguls. They can be impatient and brusque, warm and witty.

Conversations are often peppered with keen observations of the world around them, and show a great sense of humor. Almost every ethnic group, every nation on earth, is represented here. The babel of accents and languages, the kaleidoscope of faces and fashions, adds to the buzz of the city. Everyone who settles in New York helps make the city what it is, bringing their skills, labor, customs and creativity.

Some immigrant groups have made a particular impact. In the 19th and early 20th centuries, waves of Irish, Jewish, and Italian immigrants came here, settling first in the tenements of the Lower East Side. As they assimilated into the city, they also made their mark on the neighborhoods—today they all have Jewish and Italian delis. Despite its sophistication, New York is a city of neighborhoods. If you want to get to know it beyond the tourist attractions, stroll through the trendy streets of Greenwich Village and the East Village, or the artsy quarters of SoHo, Chelsea, and TriBeCa. Of the numerous ethnic neighborhoods, Chinatown, Little Italy, Harlem, and El Barrio are the best known, but there are dozens of other enclaves where families from Greece, Poland, Korea, and elsewhere have gathered, such as the Russian immigrants of Brooklyn's Brighton Beach. These are some of the most colorful pockets of the city, and like everything else in New York, they are constantly reinventing themselves.

Since the 1960s, most newcomers have come from Asia, the Caribbean, and Latin America, particularly Puerto Rico. Today Hispanics are the second largest ethnic group, numbering around 27 percent of the population. Latino food, language, and music adds another beat to the city's rhythm. As so many nationalities call New York home, you'll find an ethnic festival or parade taking place every month of the year. Some of the largest celebrations, such as Chinese New Year, St. Patrick's Day, or the Feast of San Gennaro in Little Italy, are world famous.

Reinvention

New York is a relatively young city. It isn't bound by tradition and is always changing, always tearing down, and building anew, embracing the next innovation. Throughout its history, buildings sturdy enough to last for centuries have often been demolished and replaced a generation later. Some downtown lots have been redeveloped as many as five times since the early 1800s. The resulting hodgepodge of styles led the Swiss architect Le Corbusier to refer to New York as 'a beautiful catastrophe.'

Few of the elegant neoclassical mansions that once graced the Upper East Side around the turn of the 20th century still stand. They were built by the Rockefellers, the Vanderbilts, and other industrial magnates, but within a few decades they were torn down to make way for department stores and apartment buildings. Historic landmarks remain, including Federal Hall, Trinity Hall, and

Over the east entrance of the prominent G.E. Building, the former RCA Building, is Lee Lawrie's limestone-and-glass frieze "Wisdom" (right).
When St. Patrick's Cathedral (far right) was built in 1878, architect James Renwick Jnr. must have had a premonition of the skyscrapers to come.

Castle Clinton, but most of New York's public buildings date from the late 19th or 20th centuries. Perhaps the greatest survivor is Grand Central Terminal, a glorious Beaux-Arts structure saved from demolition in the 1970s and restored, after a public awakening to the value of its architectural past.

Think of New York architecture, and you immediately picture its soaring skyline—sightseeing in New York often involves looking up. Although the first skyscraper was erected in Chicago in the late 19th century, New York took this building style to heart and made it into an art form. Within a century the skyscrapers of New York City had created one of the world's most memorable skylines. Most of these spectacular tall buildings are clustered around the financial district of Lower Manhattan and in Midtown where the great art deco masterpieces, the Chrysler Building and the Empire State Building, have become symbols of the city. Styles have evolved over the years, from the ornate to the ultramodern.

Iconic New York

Many landmark attractions are cultural icons, not only of the city but of the nation and even the world. Foremost of these is the Statue of Liberty, a World Heritage Site and a symbol of freedom around the globe. It was a gift from France to the United States in commemoration of shared democratic ideals and their alliance during the American War of Independence. Since its installation on Liberty Island in New York Harbor in 1886, it has welcomed generations of new arrivals to America's shores.

The Brooklyn Bridge is arguably the most famous bridge in the country apart from San Francisco's Golden Gate Bridge. Completed in 1883, it was the world's first steel suspension bridge. Its massive towers and wire cables are still a thing of beauty, and its walkway provides one of the finest views of Lower Manhattan.

More garish, but no less a symbol of New York, is the neon-lit, billboard-plastered Times Square. Generations of Americans have, via their television screens if not in person, celebrated the New Year by counting down the seconds to midnight, when a glowing ball drops from the Times Tower.

But New York isn't just about the sights; it's about experiences. A walk through Central Park, window-shopping on Fifth Avenue, a ride on the Staten Island ferry—are quintessential New York experiences that will never go out of style. Don't limit yourself to Manhattan; the outer boroughs are rich in sights, sounds, and culture.

Art and artists

If you want to spread your wings, try your luck, use your imagination, be yourself, this is the place to do it. New York has long been a city of nonconformists, attracting mavericks, bohemians, and entrepreneurs. People come hoping to achieve their dream, or create a lifestyle. Nowhere is this more true than in the arts. Countless writers, artists, actors, and musicians have found inspiration in the city, and portrayed it in all its guises from the Hudson River school, through Jackson Pollock to Andy Warhol and Roy Lichenstein who launched the Pop Art movement in New York in the 1960s.

New York is one of the foremost art centers in the world, particularly for contemporary art. Of its many outstanding museums, the big four are the enormous Metropolitan Museum of Art, the Museum of Modern Art, the Whitney Museum of American Art, and the Guggenheim, whose circular design is a masterpiece in itself. You can add to that, the exquisite Frick Collection, housed in the elegant mansion of its industrialist benefactor, the Brooklyn Museum of Art, and hundreds of small galleries displaying contemporary and experimental works.

New York, New York

Broadway is not just synonymous with New York's theater district; it represents the pinnacle of success for theater nationwide. New York was the birthplace of the musical, beginning with Ziegfeld's *Follies* in the early 19th century, through the musicals of Rodgers and Hammerstein, to the archetypal New York musical, *West Side Story (1957)*.

New York is awash with glamour and spectacle, a celebrity in her own right. She has starred in so many films and television programs that many of her streets and buildings seem instantly familiar. From *Breakfast at Tiffany's* to *Midnight Cowboy, King Kong* to *Annie Hall, The Godfather* to *Gangs of New York*, filmmakers have given us unforgettable images of the city. It is a favorite location for many top directors, and New York is the second largest production center in the country after Hollywood.

And where would New York be without all that jazz? In the 1920s, African-American culture flourished in Harlem. In nightclubs such as the Cotton Club and the Apollo Theatre, Duke Ellington, Charlie Parker, and other music legends took jazz beyond its Southern roots, creating new styles and establishing New York as a world jazz center. The city's popular nickname—The Big Apple—was originally the name of a Harlem nightclub.

Enterprise and power

Since that first real estate transaction in the early 17th century, New York has been a land of opportunity. Where other early American colonies were founded on religious grounds, the prime objective for the Dutch trading company that governed New York was to encourage trade. In the 19th century, New York became the hub of operations for the so-called robber barons, billionaires who made their fortunes in such industries as banking, oil, railroads, and steel.

Manhattan is the headquarters for many of the largest and most powerful international companies. Above all, it is a center of high finance. Fortunes are made—and lost—on Wall Street, where the New York Stock Exchange, the largest in the world, is one of the leading drivers of the global economy. Much of the city's high adrenalin is generated in the concrete canyons of the financial district, where modern-day tycoons strike deals for sensational sums, and new schemes and scandals become the talk of the town.

Eavesdrop long enough at any bar or lunch counter and the conversation might well turn to politics. A city as diverse as New York has many rival interests, and New Yorkers are both opinionated and generally well-informed on local issues.

New York style

Style and attitude are synonymous with New York. Every leading designer has an emporium in its uptown shopping district, while downtown the hottest young designers are making their names in loft-style showrooms. From the 1930s to the 1950s, the garment industry was the largest in the city, and clothes were cut and sewn in the busy garment district around Herald Square. Here, too, is Macy's, one of New York's oldest department stores and possibly the biggest in the world. New York is famous for its department stores, with Bloomingdale's, Barneys, and Saks Fifth Avenue among the

other household names. Although the clothing manufacturing business has moved out of the city, shopping remains a mainstay of the economy. There are thousands of stores in New York, from bargain basement to haute couture.

Most of America's major publishers are based in New York, attracting top international authors and journalists. In a country where there is no serious national newspaper, the *New York Times* and the *Wall Street Journal* are regarded as the heavyweights of the journalism world. Advertising and marketing, real estate, banking, insurance, and tourism are other leading industries in the city.

Sport and leisure

New York's love of baseball is legendary. Ever since Babe Ruth set a record with 60 home runs in 1927 for the New York Yankees, Yankee Stadium is the place to be during baseball season, particularly for games with the rival New York team, the Mets. Other hot tickets include the New York Knicks for basketball fans, and the New York Giants and New York Jets football games.

For participatory sport, Central Park is New York's great, green oasis, the place where you'd go for a relaxing stroll or a calorie-burning run. Horseback riding, cycling, rollerblading, and boating on the lake are all possible in the heart of the city. In winter there is ice-skating, here and at the ice rink at Rockefeller Center. The waterfront has become the latest recreational hotspot, with a 28-mile (45km) cycle path, a new waterfront park and promenade, and fishing, sailing, and kayaking from renovated piers.

Rhythm and color

New York, observed the writer John Updike, is many cities. It's the high life of Park Avenue and the low life of the Bowery, the wheeling on Orchard Street, and the dealing on Wall Street, a hot dog from a street vendor and soufflé at the Four Seasons. Whatever you're looking for, you can find it in New York.

This is a city of many moods. Its rhythms ebb and flow. The stampede of the commuter rushes, the adrenalin surges of the business day, give way to the exciting sensations and camaraderie of the night. The city can be stimulating, exhausting, romantic. It's the green of Central Park, the gray of the concrete buildings, the blue reflections in the skyscrapers, pink neon lights, yellow taxi cabs, a rainbow of faces. These are the colors of New York, always a spectacle, always exhilarating.

The lighting of the Christmas tree at Rockefeller Center in the first week of December marks the start of the festive season. Christmas lights sparkle on buildings and trees throughout the city and snow falls as shoppers rush to collect last-minute presents.

CAFÉ CULTURE

No other place in the world offers such a range of culinary experiences. This is the city that invented cheesecake, egg creams, bagels, Reuben sandwiches, Waldorf salad, and the humble hot dog. The flavors of New York spring from its immigrants, old and new, who over the decades have introduced the recipes of their homelands to the metropolis. From tiny backstreet kitchens to the showplaces of some of the world's top chefs, New York cuisine is the essence of gastronomic fusion. Eating out is a way of life in the city's delis and diners, coffee shops and coffee bars, venerable dining rooms and hip hotspots.

There are thousands of restaurants in the city, places for sustenance and socializing. New Yorkers spend much of their valuable free time in restaurants, seeing and being seen, enjoying the contrasting flavors of their city. Greek, Italian, Indian, Caribbean, Japanese, Thai—there are dishes from around the world, plus home-grown American fare. Café culture operates round the clock. A seafood meal in Chelsea (left) begins before dawn, at the counters of Fulton Fish Market, which has supplied the city's restaurants since 1834 from South Street Seaport. Now trendy eateries fill the renovated warehouses that line the seaport's piers (above right). New Yorkers may wait weeks to taste the creations of the latest celebrity chef, but everyone has a favorite neighborhood stalwart.

New York's culinary temples can be found in unexpected places. The famous Oyster Bar (above) is set on the lower concourse of Grand Central Terminal. Beneath the shiny golden tiles of its vaulted ceiling, diners feast on plates of fresh fish and oysters on the half shell, oblivious to the commuter rush outside the walls. The Empire Diner is a cultural icon, its gleaming chrome walls announcing the art deco wonderland within. This is the classic American diner of the 1920s at its best, open 24 hours and a popular hangout for the hip, young clubbing crowd of West Chelsea.

The city is always on the move. It's the ultimate fast-food center. Breakfast and lunch are often eaten on the run, but here fast food doesn't mean junk food. Munch on a deli sandwich piled high with pastrami, a bagel with lox (salmon) and a smear of cream cheese, or a fresh garden salad; roll up a slice of pizza in Little Italy, pick a pickle from the barrel on Essex Street; wake up with a steaming cup of gourmet coffee from a curbside vendor, or cool down with an icy snow-cone topped with fruity flavors.

The city is, quite literally, a movable feast. Pushcarts are piled high with huge, chewy pretzels, served hot and salted. At lunchtime, street vendors cater to the financial district and other busy workplaces from falafel carts, rolling noodle bars with steaming trays of oriental dishes, soup, and

salad bars on wheels. The flavors of New York are to be found on every street corner. The classic New York fast food is the hot dog. Invented by Charles Feltman in 1874 at his Coney Island restaurant, it was brought to the masses by one of his employees, a young German immigrant named Nathan Handwerker. Nathan's Famous is still a Coney Island specialty, but today you can bite into a dog, rolled into a bun with all the trimmings, on many a Manhattan street corner.

MARKETS

Even in the heart of Manhattan, New Yorkers find a taste of the country in the city's greenmarkets which take place at various locations on different days of the week. The largest and most famous operates four days a week at Union Square. Farmers bring their produce into the city from smallholdings in the rural areas of Long Island, the Hudson Valley, and as far away as Pennsylvania and New Jersey. Among the makeshift stalls are such treats as homemade preserves and jams, hand-pressed cider, and local honey, some specially made with the market in mind, such as New York City Roof Top Honey (above left). Stalls are piled with homemade breads, cakes and pastries (above center), organic meats and cheeses, fresh herbs and spicy chilis (above right).

Seasonal produce, much of it organically grown, is always in demand. Sweet yellow bell peppers (above left), bright orange pumpkins, dark red strawberries, spiky green artichokes, all make their seasonal debuts. Flowers such as these bright yellow sunflowers (above right) and plants are also on sale. There are around 16 greenmarkets in Manhattan alone, and a dozen more in the outer boroughs. Many are held all year round, others between May and December.

Beneath the glare of neon signs, cooked poultry dangles in the windows of dozens of Chinese restaurants. Market stalls are piled with mysterious items—animal, vegetable, or mineral? Whatever! Take a plunge and try something new.

$3.99/LB. (磅)

公魚乾

(細)

DRIED FISH

$15.50/LB. (磅)

銀魚乾

DRIED FISH

特價 $0.99/LB. 磅

黑棗

特價 $2.99/LB

寧夏杞子

$42.50/LB. (磅)

日本宗谷

江瑤柱

DRIED SCALLOP

特價 $48.50/LB 磅

特大宗谷元貝碎

Nowhere are the flavors of New York more exotic than in Chinatown, the heart of the city's Chinese community since the 1870s. The original area expanded quickly in the 1960s when a relaxation of immigration rules permitted more Asian immigration. This densely populated quarter is teeming with vibrant colors, pungent smells, and a range of Asian dialects. The streets are a jigsaw puzzle of herbalist shops, dim sum houses, restaurants, bustling markets, bargain stores, banks, signs in Chinese characters. The scene is as striking as this display in a shop window (above).

DELIS

New York has some unique dining institutions, the most famous of which is the deli. Jewish delis are the most traditional, selling a vaiety of smoked fishes and meats plus bagels, pastrami, and corned beef sandwiches, chopped liver, pickles and knishes.

The deli is a New York institution. There are more here than anywhere else in the country and they range from tiny neighborhood groceries to gourmet food markets such as Balducci's on Sixth Avenue (above left), which also has a popular café. Delis are a legacy of two major immigrant groups who settled in New York's Lower East Side. At a traditional Jewish deli you can try such legendary specialties as matzo ball (dumpling) soup, blintzes, knishes (a doughy pastry filled with potatoes), gefilte fish (whitefish), bagels, lox (salmon), pastrami or corned beef on rye. Italian delis, like this one in Little Italy (right) bulge with spicy salamis, cured meats, ham, delicious creamy cheeses, homemade pastas, tubs of olives, and oils.

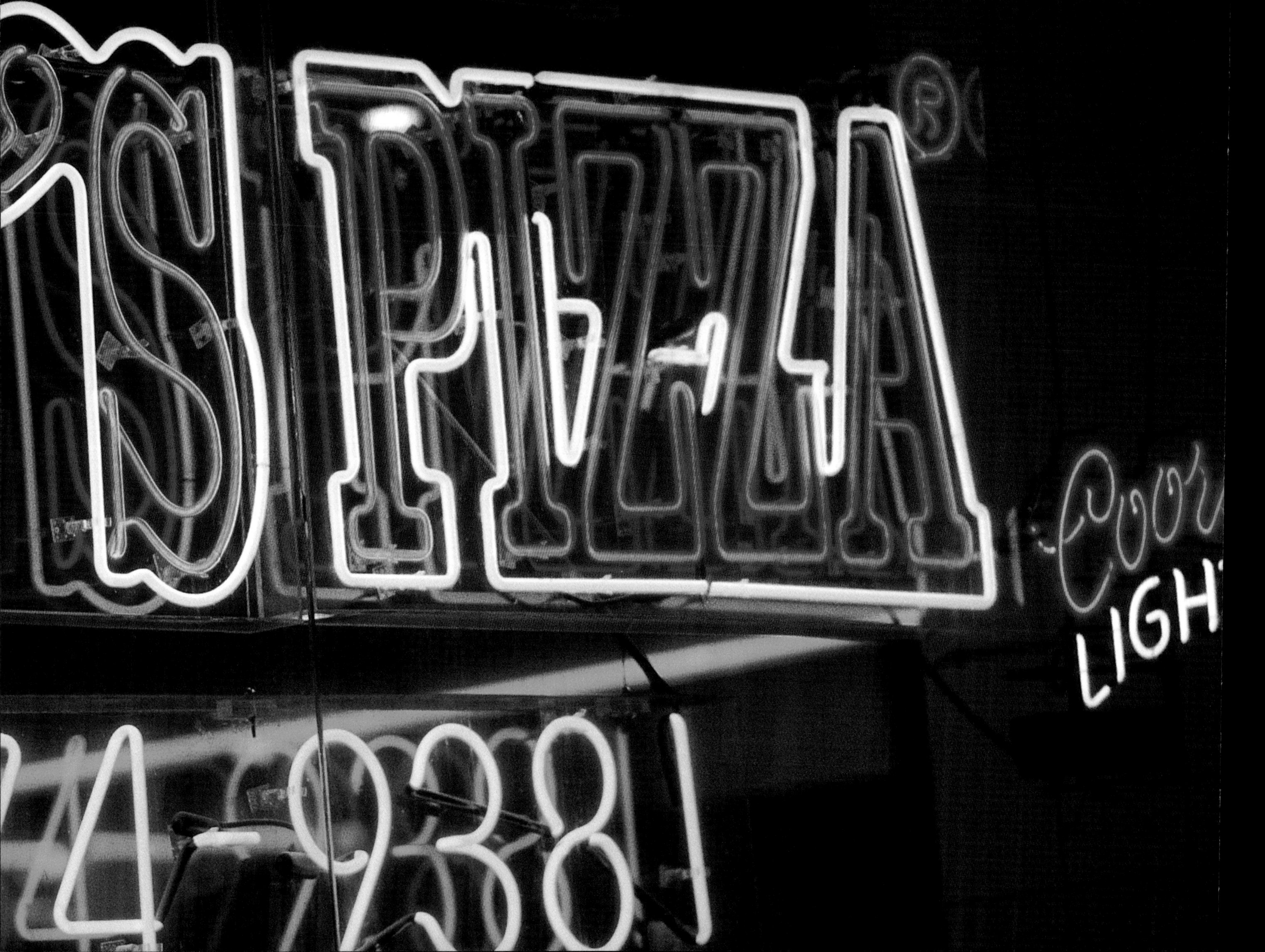
S PIZZA
Coor
LIGH
4 238

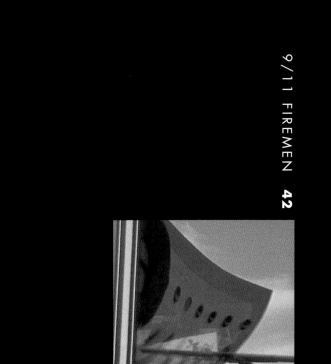

COLORS OF NEW YORK: **LIFE & PEOPLE**

2

ARRIVALS AND DEPARTURES

Every day, around half a million people move through Grand Central Terminal (above left). The elegance of its Beaux-Arts architecture is a monument to rail travel and to the unending lure of New York. Find a quiet spot and admire the vast main concourse, with its soaring arched windows, marble floor, and grand staircase, and 125-foot (38m) high vaulted ceiling covered in lighted zodiac constellations. It is said to be the largest room in the world. But this isn't just a rail terminal. As well as shops, cafés, and restaurants, it is home to the celebrated Oyster Bar & Restaurant.

On the main concourse, the four-faced brass clock of the information booth (above right) marks the time for people dispersing in all directions. More than 35 million visitors come to New York every year, and plot their own course through the city.

Few people forget their first arrival in New York. Whether we come for business, pleasure, or to make a new life, we carry preconceptions along with our baggage. Photographs, films, and television have given us thousands of images of life in the city. We approach it with a mixture of awe and excitement.

The first thing you notice is the pace. Traffic and pedestrians rush by, eyes ahead, but aware of everything around them. Soon, you too are swept up into the exhilarating flow of life and people that is New York City.

This is a city of aspirations. People come here seeking to fulfil a dream, whether that dream is making a killing on Wall Street or a splash on Madison Avenue, becoming a star on stage, or a citizen in a new land. If you can make it in New York, as the song says, you can make it anywhere.

All New Yorkers are part of this surge of coming and going which renews the city daily. This doorman at the 1905 Beaux-Arts Peninsula Hotel on Fifth Avenue (left), is witness to the action.

Following pages: Grand Central Terminal

9/11 FIREMEN

Every day there are a million small, personal triumphs in New York. On September 11, 2001, there was one great national tragedy. Terrorists flew airplanes into the twin towers of the World Trade Center, symbol of the city's dominance and success. In the hours and days that followed, the firefighters (right), police, medical, and other emergency workers became the city's grim heroes. Nearly 3,000 people lost their lives. Flowers, flags, messages, and prayers were laid near the site as the nation mourned. The towers fell, but the city's spirit remained undaunted. Soon, a new monument will rise from the ashes of Ground Zero. But New York and the world will never forget.

POSH SHOPS

New York is one of the world's great fashion capitals. Style is an important element in city life, whether for formal, business, or casual wear. There are more than 10,000 stores in the city, and many people come to New York just to shop. All the world's top designers, from Armani and agnés b. (above left) to Yamamoto and Yves St. Laurent have their own shops in the city. Many are clustered along Madison Avenue, the ultra-chic shopping street on the Upper East Side. Home-grown designers such as Donna Karan and Calvin Klein showcase their designs around the world.

Famous for its department stores, a visit to NYC isn't complete without a browse through Saks Fifth Avenue (above left), Barneys, Macy's, or Bloomingdale's. Almost everywhere you go in midtown Manhattan, a stylish window display beckons you inside.

The city's small, cutting-edge boutiques offer some of the most interesting fashions. Hot designers moved into trendy loft-style stores in SoHo (above right). When the rents in their ultra-fashionable warehouse-style stores became too expensive, many moved to NoLita (North of Little Italy).

New York's greatest asset is its people. They provide the energy, the drive, and the variety that make the city so fascinating. In Columbus Park in Chinatown, residents gather for friendly games of Chinese chess (above left) or *mah jongg*.

New York is truly a rainbow city, home to people of all races, nationalities, and creeds. Out of a population of eight million, just over 38 percent are white, 27 percent are Latino, 25 percent are African American and 10 percent are Asian. Nearly every nation on earth is represented in this vibrant, multicultural melting pot. There are more than 39,000 police officers in New York, and many ethnic minorities count themselves among New York's Finest. In the East Village, a Hispanic policeman shares a joke with a colleague (above right).

NEW YORK AMERICANS

Immigrants have always kept the city moving. Many newcomers find jobs in hotels (above left) and restaurants, or other service industries. Throughout the boroughs, New York's ethnic enclaves are always growing, changing, moving on, and making room for a new generation.

In the 19th century, the Lower East Side became home to thousands of Jewish people fleeing persecution in Russia and Eastern Europe. Today, New York has the largest Jewish community outside of Israel (above right).

As the people prospered, so the city did too, absorbing their foods, feast days, and phrases into the rhythms of New York life. It has been this way for the Irish, Italians, Puerto Ricans, and many other incomers over the decades.

Whether they've lived here all their lives, or only for a short time, New Yorkers are proud of their city and their country. Stickers with American flags adorn car bumpers, windows, and even hard hats (left). The city's great symbol of freedom, the Statue of Liberty, was once the first thing immigrants saw when they sailed into New York Harbor. This man (above) gets into the spirit on Liberty Island with his own souvenir crown. A sense of humor is part of the American spirit.

With its stunning skyline and its variety of grand and gritty urban backdrops, New York is a natural movie set. It ranks as the second largest production center in the United States. Director Martin Scorsese delved into the mean streets, while Woody Allen captures the city's quirkiness and romance.

The number of big movie productions here has mushroomed in recent years. Add to that dozens of television shows, and there's a good chance of coming across a film shoot any day of the year (above left).

At work or play, New York is a place of energy and activity. There's a survival instinct in the air, an eye for opportunity. New Yorkers may sometimes seem brusque and hurried, but they're quick-witted, too, with a wry sense of humor that comes from a sharp awareness of everything around them.

WORK, REST, AND PLAY

The city attracts people with their own personal vision, who express themselves and live life as they see it. From the late, flamboyant writer and ex-British civil servant Quentin Crisp to Madonna, people have come here from afar and carved out new identities.

Conquering such a solidly urban environment requires ingenuity. But there are many ways to rest the mind and the soul. Wall Street traders find time for a game of chess on the street (above). Look closely and you'll see gardens on rooftops and in vacant lots, verdant corners where

neighbors socialize and couples can be alone. Central Park is New York's great oasis, the playground for the entire city and at 843 acres it offers plenty of space for rollerbladers, skateboarders, cyclists, joggers, dog-walkers, sun-bathers, and more to find recreation and renewal.

WALL STREET

Wall Street, in the heart of New York's financial district, is the powerhouse of the nation. Behind the Corinthian columns of its neoclassical façade, fortunes rise and fall on the trading floor of the

The stock market today is a far cry from its origins in the 18th century, when the first brokers made their deals here under a buttonwood tree, but stressed financiers (above) still seek out a spot of

From a pedestal outside Federal Hall, a statue of George Washington (right) gazes towards that hub of global finance, the New York Stock Exchange. During their lunch break, workers lounge on the

ARCHITE

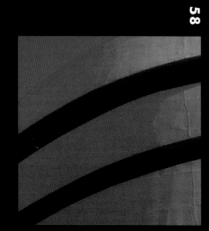

COLORS OF NEW YORK: **ARCHITECTURE**

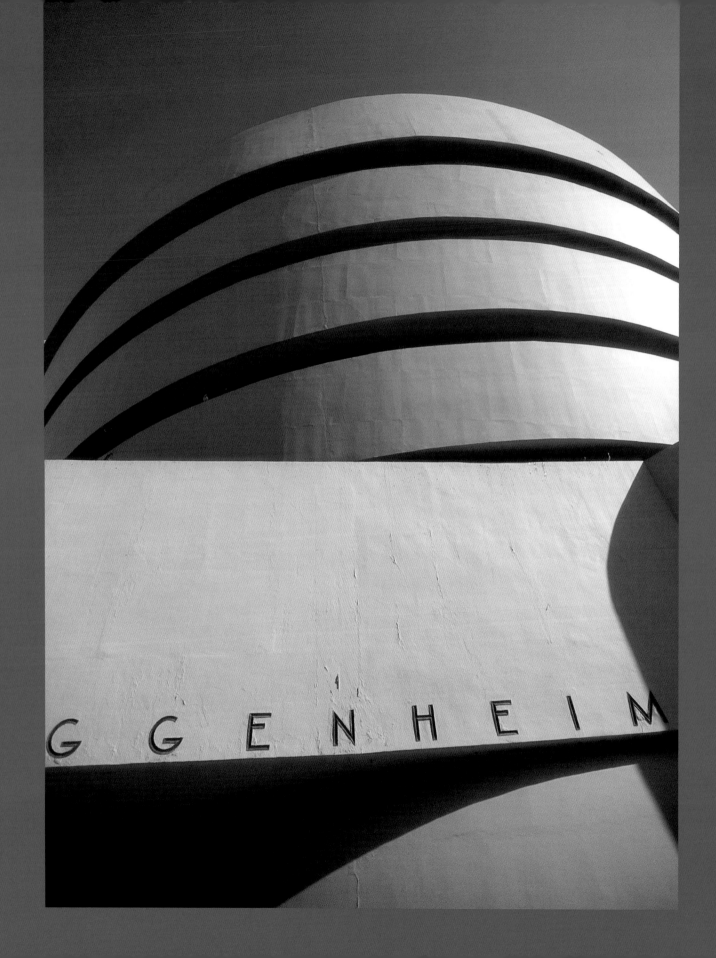

DESIGN DETAILS

Buildings in Europe stand for centuries. In New York, you can watch them come and go within your lifetime. Manhattan refuses to let itself be hemmed in on its narrow island. It makes room for the spirited new idea, the bold statement, by pulling things down and building up all over again.

The city's architecture is eclectic, embracing both tradition and innovation. The ornate details of its grand old monuments butt up against the cool, clean lines of modern commercial towers. New York may be famous for its skyscrapers, but it shows its other faces in the Beaux-Arts elegance of the Public Library, the cast-iron facades of SoHo, its neighborhood brownstones, tenements, and row houses, and the ecclesiastical splendor of its churches.

Previous pages: Guggenheim Museum
New York loves originality and flair. The massive white curves of the Guggenheim Museum's circular exterior form a unique façade that contrasts the sharp vertical lines of the surroundings buildings. Finished in the year of his death, it is the metropolitan masterpiece of architect Frank Lloyd Wright (1867–1959). Inside, works of modern art are displayed along a spiral ramp that winds up and around the six-story atrium, creating a radically different viewing experience that Wright believed was more natural to the eye.

Few skyscrapers are more loved than William van Alen's Chrysler Building, over 70 years old and still the height of art deco style. Its shimmering stainless-steel spire is one of the city's most famous landmarks.

BRIDGES

The Brooklyn Bridge, the world's first steel
suspension bridge, was a great feat of engineering.
Its soaring Gothic double arches at either end were
built as portals to Brooklyn and New York, then
separate cities. Architect John Augustus Roebling
died following an accident and his son Washington
continued the work.

Native Americans crossed the Hudson River in canoes. Early Dutch settlers used rowboats. Today more than 105 million vehicles cross it every year on the George Washington Bridge (above and right). Opened in 1931, less than 50 years after the Brooklyn Bridge, it is now the busiest bridge in the world, a thoroughfare for vehicles and pedestrians, joggers and rollerbladers.

Of the six major bridges into Manhattan, these two are the most graceful, Brooklyn with its mile-long web of steel cables, the George Washington with its diamond necklace of mercury vapor lights.

Like the masses of people on the street, Manhattan's skyscrapers are striving to impose their identity. Their tops were often modeled on classical monuments to make them stand out. However, the triangular shape of Daniel Burnham's Flatiron Building (left) made it a Fifth Avenue landmark.

SKYSCRAPERS

The Empire State Building (left), finished in 1931, was the world's tallest building for over 40 years. The panoramic views from its 86th-floor observation deck take in the Chrysler Building and United Nations building (above) and are especially romantic at night (overleaf).

INTERIORS

In New York you can find any environment to suit your mood. The glass-walled Trump Tower, built in the 1980s by tycoon Donald Trump, is a monument to affluence inside and out. Pink marble, mirrors, shrubbery, and a waterfall decorate the showy atrium (left) lined with designer boutiques.

The Reading Room of the New York Public Library (above) on Fifth Avenue offers a retreat from the rush outside. The 1911 library was designed by the firm of Carrère and Hastings. The Reading Room is two blocks long and has ceiling murals, chandeliers, brass table lamps, and oak paneling.

From the tenements of the Lower East Side to the
luxury apartments of the Upper West Side—Dakota,
Beresford, Eldorado, San Remo, Century—New
York's neighborhoods exhibit an interesting array
of urban architecture in a physical reflection of the
city's history. Little survives from the colonial era,
but the 19th-century Greek Revival row houses and
Italianate brownstones of the residential areas are
highly prized. Fire was once a danger in the
cramped tenements of Lower Manhattan, but the
zigzag fire escapes now form a distinctive feature
of the cityscape.

Cast-iron buildings made their debut in the mid-19th century in Manhattan's commercial quarter. This innovation allowed façades with ornamental details to be prefabricated from molds, bolted together and erected cheaply. New York has the world's largest concentration of this type of industrial architecture. Some of the best examples, such as the Staples Building on Spring Street (above left) can be seen in the SoHo Cast-Iron Historic District.

CHURCHES

New York's churches display some of its most glorious architecture and superlative interiors. Trinity Church on Wall Street, built in 1846, introduced the Gothic Revival style to many of the city's religious buildings. The finest example is St. Patrick's Cathedral, the largest Catholic cathedral in the United States, whose massive bronze doors (above left) hold statues of the saints of New York, including Elizabeth Ann Seton; the two spires rise 300 feet into the sky. It was designed by James Renwick, Jr., who was inspired by the great European cathedrals. Another is Riverside Church (left), funded by John D. Rockefeller and modeled after Chartres Cathedral. Its 21-story bell tower (above center) houses the world's largest carillon, with 74 bells. The Cathedral of St. John the Divine in Morningside Heights, begun in 1892 and still uncompleted, is the world's largest Gothic church.

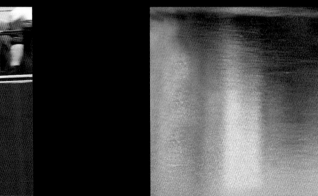

COLORS OF NEW YORK:
LANDMARKS & VIEWS

4

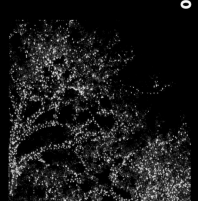

STATUE OF LIBERTY

New York is a city of landmarks. Some, such as the Statue of Liberty, are symbols of the entire nation. Designed by the French sculptor Frédéric-Auguste Bartholdi and constructed by engineer Gustav Eiffel as a monument to American independence, her official title is *Liberty Enlightening the World*. City dwellers have other, less lofty landmarks that likewise are symbols of city life, from the glitter of Times Square to the green swathe of Central Park to the amusements of Coney Island.

Up close, the cityscape may be a mixture of the good, the bad, and the ugly, but its sum is far greater than its parts. Seen from offshore or, even better, from above, the Manhattan skyline is a truly spectacular sight.

Lady Liberty stands an impressive 151 feet (46m) from the top of the base to the tip of her torch, and weights 225 tons/tonnes. Her torch symbolizes enlightenment, while the seven rays of her crown stand for the seven seas and the seven continents.

Central Park, the city's 'great green lung,' was created by Frederick Law Olmsted and Calvert Vaux in 1858 from a derelict area of pig farms, quarries, and squatters' camps. It runs for 50 blocks between Manhattan's Upper East and Upper West sides, a rectangular oasis of meadows, gardens, lakes,

woodland, playing fields, and terraces, with 58 miles (95km) of paths for jogging and cycling. This landmark gives New Yorkers expansive natural views in the heart of the city.

Pretty Bow Bridge (left) spans The Lake and is one of the park's seven original cast-iron bridges. It links to the Ramble (right), a rustic, wooded area of footpaths and streams that is ideal for birdwatching. On Sunday afternoons (above), Central Park is the city's playground.

CENTRAL PARK

Previous Page: Midtown Manhattan at dusk from Central Park

Venturing beyond Manhattan opens up your view of New York. The outer boroughs contain several lesser known but highly interesting landmarks, and paint a broader picture of life beyond the frenetic city. Relics of colonial times survive in the Van Cortlandt House in the Bronx, and the historic buildings of Richmond Town on Staten Island. Though parts of the Bronx are often associated with urban decay, the borough also has two of the city's finest green spaces—the New York Botanical Garden and the Bronx Zoo—as well as New York's sporting landmark, Yankee Stadium. In Queens, Flushing Meadows-Corona Park was the site of two World's Fairs (1939 and 1964), whose buildings now house the New York Hall of Science and the Queens Museum of Art.

BOTANIC GARDENS

Brooklyn is arguably the most attractive of the outer boroughs, with New York's second-largest art museum and beautiful Prospect Park, designed by the creators of Central Park. Brooklyn Botanic Gardens is a pleasant retreat, with more than 13,000 varieties of plants from around the world.

In spring cherry blossoms (left) along the esplanade are a popular attraction. An elegant palm house and modern greenhouses (above), water-lily ponds, and a rose garden are other highlights, while the Japanese hill-and-pond garden (bottom right) features Shinto shrines and a tea house.

CONEY ISLAND

Another Brooklyn highlight is the legendary Coney Island, once known as the Playground of the World. Here, a day by the seaside is a short subway ride from Manhattan. For more than a century Coney Island's amusement park rides have offered cheap thrills for millions of visitors, who stroll along the boardwalk enjoying the breezy ocean views while eating cotton candy, hamburgers, and Nathan's Famous hot dogs. There are great views of Manhattan from the wooden Wonder Wheel (right), built in 1920 and still the world's tallest Ferris wheel at 150 feet (46m). But things started even earlier. A series of pavilions for sea bathing and the Iron Pier opened in the 1870s and 1880s, followed by luxury seaside hotels. Earlier parks have long since disappeared and today's generation finds their thrills at Astroland.

The panoramic view from the 86th-floor observation deck of the Empire State Building is always memorable, especially at night. Here, the office blocks of Chelsea and the Garment District are a twinkling mass of lights set against a darkening purple sky.

The trees are aglow with hundreds of tiny lights at the Tavern on the Green in Central Park. Originally a sheepfold, it was built in 1870 as a home for the 200 sheep that grazed the Sheep Meadow.

ADIO CITY
RADIO CITY CHRISTMAS SPECTACULAR 11/7 -
"WE'LL DRIVE YOU HAPPY"
PANORAMA

AT

ICONS

Art, culture, and style are bywords for New York. From individual expression on the city streets to acclaimed works on the international stage, these are the elements that give the city its special panache. New York is the leading center in the country for arts and entertainment, from music and dance to theater and galleries. It has benefited from the generosity of many wealthy patrons who have amassed outstanding art collections and ploughed much of their fortunes back into the city's cultural institutions, which are some of the finest in the nation. New York has given birth to many icons of culture and style; but it also inspires rebellion and innovation, from street art to Pop Art, street cred to cutting-edge fashion and design.

New York is full of the icons of American life. From an elevated platform high above Duffy Square, workers clean a model of a Coca-Cola bottle. New York is at the center of the nation's advertising industry, responsible for generating many worldwide trends.

Some of New York's most artistic touches can be seen in unexpected places, brightening up the dullest corners of the city. Even a humble fire hydrant can be painted up in style.

Baseball is as American as apple pie. Uncle Sam's top hat crowns the tip of a baseball bat on this sign in Times Square for the home team, the New York Yankees.

New York's yellow cabs are an unmissable symbol of the city, recognized around the world. They have appeared in movies (in *Taxi Driver*, 1976, starring Robert DeNiro), on TV (the late 1970s cult series *Taxi* starring Danny DeVito), and even works of art (Mondrian's *Broadway Boogie Woogie*, 1942/3, where they appeared as small yellow rectangles). John Hertz founded the Yellow Cab Company in 1907, choosing the bright signature hue after a survey deemed it the color most easy to spot. Today more than 12,000 cabs cruise the streets of New York, but many New Yorkers find it preferable to walk, especially during one of the city's notorious gridlocks. These days, cell phones have taken over from the once familiar phone booth for communication-on-the-go.

ACCESSORIES

If you can't find what you want in New York, it probably doesn't exist. Shopping is not a mere necessity in the city; it's an art form, and there are stores across the city to fit everyone's style and budget. Browse the trendy shops of Greene Street, SoHo, for decorative glassware, lamps, and other accessories for the home (left and top right). NoLita (*North of Little Italy*) is the city's latest style quarter. The boutiques here are a fun place to shop for bags, shoes, hats, jewelry, and other accessories. For a more ostentatious environment, take your credit card uptown to the Trump Tower.

Express yourself! This phrase seems to be the motto of New York. Even the city walls become canvases for artists wanting to display their creativity or send a message outside the mainstream media. What began in the 1970s as hip-hop graffiti with its cryptic tags and colorful spraycan lettering evolved into a higher revolutionary statement known as street art, made famous by New York artists Jean-Michel Basquiat and Keith Haring. Today there is so much street art on the walls and sidewalks of Lower Manhattan that the urban landscape is a virtual museum.

If there was a way to tally all the murals, graphics, cartoons, sketches, scribbles, stencils, stickers, and posters by unknown street artists, no one would be surprised if the result equalled or even outnumbered all the recognized works of art in the galleries and museums for which the city is famous.

STREET ART

Street art is grounded in its neighborhood. George Segal's sculpture *Gay Liberation* (far left) was installed in Christopher Park, a gay area, in 1992. Nearby, a wall graphic by an anonymous artist (left) depicts laughter, rage, excitement—whatever emotion the eye beholds.

In the rundown neighborhoods of Harlem, street artists improve their surroundings with murals that celebrate community culture and commemorate local heroes (above top). Trendy stores in Chelsea (above bottom) and SoHo enlist graffiti artists to give their premises an artsy edge.

New York has more than 1,000 art galleries, ranging from the well-known, world-class museums of the Uptown to the private, cutting-edge galleries of Lower Manhattan. Wealthy patrons, such as the sculptor Gertrude Vanderbilt Whitney (1877–1942), founder of the Whitney Museum of American Art (above left), have been instrumental in establishing the city as an international art center. They not only amassed their own personal collections and founded museums for the enjoyment of the public, but also supported and encouraged unknown artists. Many of Whitney's protégés, such as Edward Hopper (1882–1967) and John Sloan (1871–1951), became major creative forces in 20th-century American art. Tomorrow's stars emerge in the warehouse galleries of SoHo and Chelsea, such as the Phyllis Kind Gallery (above right).

The airy Great Hall of the Metropolitan Museum of Art with planters and the central information desk where you can ask for a museum plan—essential to find your way around the galleries.

PERFORMING ART

Sometimes you'll find art outside the museum as well as inside. Colorful banners announce the current exhibitions at many cultural institutions such as the Metropolitan Museum of Art or the American Museum of Natural History.

The Lincoln Center (above) on Manhattan's Upper West Side, is New York's premier institution for the performing arts. With 14 venues, it hosts concerts of jazz and classical music, world-renowned opera and ballet companies, and the annual New York Film Festival.

LN
CTER

Marsalis
irector

3
N

THE
CHAMBER
MUSIC
SOCIETY OF
LINCOLN
CENTER
2002-03
SEASON AT ALICE TULLY HALL
DAVID SHIFRIN, ARTISTIC DIRECTOR

THE NATION'S PREMIER REPERTORY
COMPANY FOR CHAMBER MUSIC
www.ChamberMusicSociety.org

40TH
SEP27
OCT13
NEW YORK
FILM
FESTIVAL

PROUDLY SPONSORED BY
Grand Marnier

Film Society of
Lincoln Center

LIGHT & REFLECTIONS

ONS

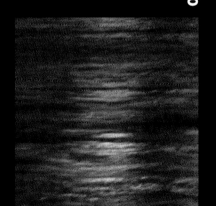

WATER **120**

SKYSCRAPERS 124

Some parts of New York, especially Times Square, appear to be built with walls of light. This section of Broadway was first lit up in the early 20th century. Its two- and three-story signs used white light bulbs, earning it the nickname 'The Great White Way.'

WALLS OF LIGHT

New York may be a man-made environment, but the urban landscape is much more than concrete canyons, painted signboards, and dreary grids of gray and brown. The city shimmers with light and reflections. By day its towering skyscrapers mirror blue skies and passing clouds. After dark, they twinkle with millions of glowing lights, an electric parade that stretches as far as the eye can see. Closer to ground level, pink, yellow, red, and orange neon signs bathe the night streets in eerie brilliance. The Manhattan skyline is reflected in the encircling shoreline and the ponds and reservoir of Central Park. All across the city, windows capture and return the round-the-clock whirlwind of faces, shapes, and colors of New York.

As Times Square rose ever higher, it was covered by brighter and brasher signage. Today it radiates with around 50 supersigns, such as the Dow Jones 'Zipper,' a digital ribbon, and the giant Coca-Cola bottle.

WINDOWS

From a coveted window seat in a restaurant or café, you can linger over coffee and watch an intriguing parade of humanity, a kaleidoscope of faces and fashions, pass by. Fleeting streaks of color from yellow cabs, red jackets, pink hair filter through the neutral glass. Window-shopping is a constant diversion. Stores beckon you in with tantalizing window displays of the latest styles and trends.

Windows also create a third dimension, a montage
of the worlds without and within. Pause to observe
New York through these reflections, and you will
see the city from a fascinating new perspective.

UPLIFTING INTERIORS

New York may seem to worship Mammon, but its spiritual side is reflected in the beauty of its churches. Step inside Grace Church in the East Village (top left), Riverside Church (bottom left) or St. Patrick's Cathedral (bottom right and above), and the burdens of the outside world are lifted by the soaring grace of the Gothic Revival architecture. Similar enlightenment can be found in the city's synagogues, mosques, and Orthodox cathedrals. The play of light through stained glass and imposing windows illuminates the richly decorated interiors of these places of worship.

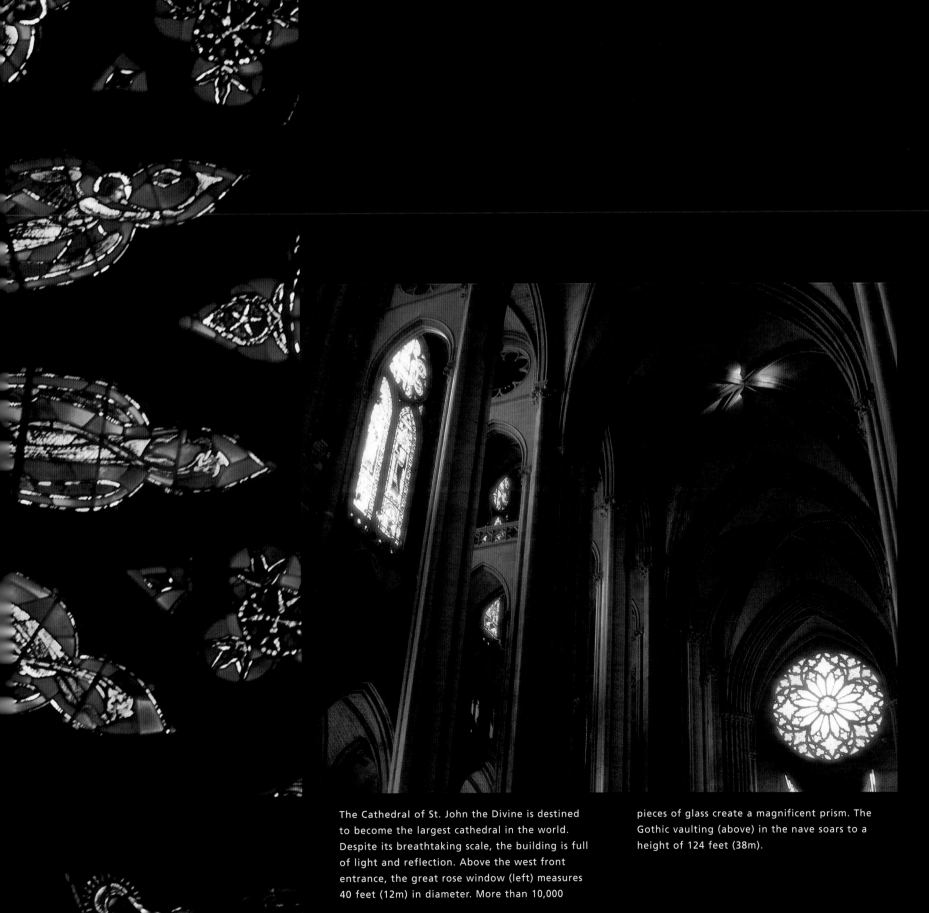

The Cathedral of St. John the Divine is destined to become the largest cathedral in the world. Despite its breathtaking scale, the building is full of light and reflection. Above the west front entrance, the great rose window (left) measures 40 feet (12m) in diameter. More than 10,000 pieces of glass create a magnificent prism. The Gothic vaulting (above) in the nave soars to a height of 124 feet (38m).

WATER

The Pond, The Lake, The Pool, The Reservoir, Conservatory Water, Harlem Mere—these are the bodies of water that punctuate the green expanses of Central Park. Perhaps the simplicity of their names reflects their role in mirroring the light and tranquillity of the open spaces around them.

Bow Bridge (above and right) is one of the loveliest of Central Park's ornamental bridges. Views of the greenery and buildings bordering the park are reflected in the waters of the lake below its graceful arch.

Manhattan is also mirrored in the East and Hudson
rivers that surround the island. The reflections of
light from the city's major bridges are an awesome
spectacle, especially at night.
Following pages: Manhattan Bridge

SKYSCRAPERS

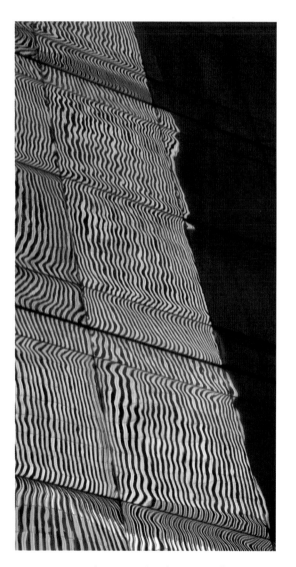

New York's first skyscraper was built in 1890 and stood for less than 30 years. Over the next century, the city constructed some of the best-loved skyscrapers in the world. As the buildings grew ever taller, residents feared that they would block out all the sunlight, turning the streets into dark canyons. Instead, new zoning laws passed in 1916 required skyscrapers to use 'setbacks,' stepping back the upper stories to allow light to penetrate to ground level. This gave the Manhattan skyscraper its distinctive look.

With the building of sleek modern towers of glass and steel, skyscrapers became enhancers of the light. Today their glimmering surfaces reflect the sunlight, the sky, and each other.

From the beginning, skyscrapers embodied the
spirit of New York. Their architects and developers
raced to be number one, and throughout the 20th
century several city skyscrapers—including the
Empire State Building—held the title of the
World's Tallest Building.

Following pages: Financial District, Lower
Manhattan

To experience New York to the full, you must take to the streets. Immerse yourself in the sights, sounds, and smells of its busy thoroughfares, and you will start to feel, rather than merely observe, the pulse of the city. There is a boundless energy here, from the commuters who swell the sidewalks during morning and evening rush hours, to the weekend power walkers in Central Park, and the clubbers spilling out of the night spots in the wee hours. With Manhattan apartments at a premium, many New Yorkers virtually live life on the streets, preferring the convenience—and variety—of food stands to sweating over a stove in a tiny kitchen, just as they love to furnish their wardrobes and living spaces with bargains from street traders and markets.

Open spaces such as Washington Square in Greenwich Village are popular hang-outs, the

ON THE STREET

New York is always on the move. In the business districts of Manhattan, time is money, and people squeeze the most out of every busy minute. Eating, working, chatting with friends, or closing a deal are often done on the move. Unlike other American cities, where the car is king, ferries, subways, buses and trains keep New York moving; but there's also a rhythm to the city's perpetual bustle. New York marks the changing seasons with annual parades and festivals, sports, and excursions beyond the city limits. It hums and throbs to an unspoken cadence from dawn till dusk and into the night.

places to go for a little urban recreation. But in New York, bicycles and rollerblades are not just for exercise—they are serious modes of transportation. Just watch the cyclists and skaters dicing with death in Fifth Avenue's rush-hour traffic, even grabbing on to passing vehicles for a free ride.

Mayor Giuliani's crackdown on crime in the 1990s gave New Yorkers a better quality of life and safer streets. A welcome change since pedestrian power propels most New Yorkers from A to B. Natural daily exercise is undoubtedly why Manhattan is arguably the slimmest borough in America.

SEASONS

The changing seasons can entice even the most resolute New Yorker beyond the city limits. In summer, many flock to the beaches of Long Island, Jones Beach, Fire Island, or the upscale retreats of the Hamptons.

North of the city, the Hudson Valley is full of historic nooks and crannies dating from colonial days. It leads to the beautiful Catskill Mountains, where the rural villages and woodlands are a prime place for soaking up the brilliant fall color.

Public transportation keeps New York moving. As with everything else in the city, there is a wide choice. The Metropolitan Transportation Authority (MTA) network is the largest transportation network in North America, covering a 5,000-square-mile (12,950sq km) area. Its subways, buses, and trains move 2.4 billion New Yorkers a year—one-third of all mass transit users in the country; MTA's bridges and tunnels carry more than 300 million vehicles a year, and buses and subways run 24 hours a day.

TRANSPORTATION

But there are many other ways to get around that offer a different travel experience. New York's famous yellow cabs provide door-to-door service. Ferries bring many workers into Manhattan each day, providing spectacular views to enliven the daily commute. Water taxis shuttle between several piers, and there are longer sightseeing cruises on the Circle Line. For open-air travel, pedicabs ply the streets of Greenwich Village, SoHo, Times Square, and other popular spots on weekends and evenings.

PARADES

New York knows how to party. In this rainbow city of immigrants from around the world, you can find an ethnic celebration taking place every month of the year. Parades are the city's forte; thousands of people regularly line the broad thoroughfare of Fifth Avenue, a popular parade route.

The most famous is Macy's Thanksgiving Day Parade. Millions of TV viewers across the country tune in to see the extravagant floats and gigantic helium balloons make their way down Central Park West and Broadway.

The biggest of New York's parades takes place on March 17, St. Patrick's Day. Tens of thousands join in the parade itself, which has been going strong for over 150 years. A week later (March 25) sees Greek Independence Day Parade, with marchers in national costume.

New Yorkers show off gaudy spring bonnets in the Easter Parade. May and June bring a memorial parade honoring Martin Luther King, the colorful Puerto Rican Day Parade with live salsa bands playing on floats, and the flamboyant Lesbian and Gay Pride Parade.

The Polish Day Parade (far left, top) takes place every October, with the outrageous Halloween Parade in Greenwich Village at the end of the month. When the marching season ends, thousands of runners come out to take part in the New York City Marathon. The route encompasses all five boroughs and ends in Central Park, with 2 million spectators lining the course to cheer the runners on their way.

FERRIES

The Staten Island Ferry is New York's best bargain. It's 5 miles (8km) from Battery Park to Staten Island, and the journey lasts 25 minutes, offering splendid views of the Statue of Liberty, Ellis Island, and the skyscrapers of Lower Manhattan—and all for free.

DAWN TILL DUSK

The vision of New York is always changing. Just as the city's rhythms vary with the ebb and flow of human activity, so its moods and atmosphere alter with the shifting light. Sunrise brings a soft, pastel glow as the metropolis slowly wakes up. The lunchtime buzz may take place under the silvery glare of the midday sun, or the slate gray of winter skies. As night falls, the city lights up, glowing like a romantic fairyland when seen from above. New York can be contrary and capricious, her temper fluctuating like the tides. Two near-identical bird's-eye views of the East River (left and above), overlooking the Manhattan and Brooklyn bridges linking the two boroughs, paint contrasting portraits of the city from dawn until dusk. They capture the ever-changing ambience, the infinite colors of New York.

CREDITS

The Automobile Association wishes to thank the following photo library and organisation for their assistance with the preparation of this book.

NYC & Company UK 132t
Photodisc 132br, 133br

The remaining photographs are held in the Automobile Association's own photo library **(AA World Travel Library)** and were taken by the following photographers:

Sarah Collier 110bc, 114t, 114b, 115; **Douglas Corrance** 3tcl, 3tcr, 5br, 9r, 23, 128br, 136; **Richard G Elliott** 10l, 55bl, 60bl, 70, 71, 77br, 90, 95bc, 99b, 106l, 107, 119, 124c, 128bc, 133cl, 134t, 134b, 134/5; **Paul Kenward** 5cl, 10r, 51tc, 54bc, 54br, 64, 66r, 77bc, 86, 88, 89, 91, 94bl, 97l, 99t, 118/9, 121, 132l, 132c, 132r, 133tl, 138r; **Nicola Lancaster** 61br; **Simon McBride** 3tr, 4br, 5bcr, 18r, 20, 22, 28t, 28/9, 30, 30/1, 35l, 36bl, 38l, 38r, 40/1, 45r, 52tr, 55bc, 56/7, 73l, 73r, 76bc, 76br, 81cl, 81cr, 82l, 82/3, 83r, 84/5, 95bl, 104r, 106r, 111bc, 122/3, 124l, 126/7, 129bc, 129br, 137tr, 140/1, 142, 142/3; **Ellen Rooney** 19c, 32t, 37bl, 49, 63r, 78, 96, 108, 111bl, 120/1, 138bl; **Clive Sawyer** 3tl, 4bl, 4bc, 5bl, 9l, 11l, 11r, 14, 16, 17tl, 17bl, 17r, 18l, 18c, 19l, 19r, 21t, 21b, 24l, 24c, 24r, 25l, 25r, 26l, 26c, 27l, 27r, 28b, 31t, 31b, 32b, 33, 34, 35r, 36bc, 36br, 37bc, 37br, 39, 42tc, 42tr, 42b, 43, 44l, 44r, 45l, 46l, 46r, 47l, 47r, 48, 50tl, 50tr, 50bl, 51r, 51b, 52tl, 52b, 53, 54bl, 55br, 58, 59, 60tl, 60tr, 60c, 60br, 61tl, 61tr, 61cl, 61c, 62, 65, 66l, 67l, 67r, 68/9, 72l, 72r, 74, 75l, 75t, 76bl, 77bl, 79, 80, 81tl, 81tr, 87tl, 87tr, 87bl, 87br, 92/3, 94bc, 94br, 97c, 97r, 98, 100t, 100l, 100cr, 100br, 101t, 101l, 101c, 101r, 102l, 102cr, 102br, 103, 104l, 105t, 105b, 108/9, 110bl, 110br, 112, 113, 116t, 116bl, 116br, 117, 124r, 125, 128bl, 129bl, 130tl, 130tr, 130bc, 131l, 131cr, 131br, 133tc, 133tr, 137tl, 137bl, 137br, 138tl, 139tr, 141t, 141b, 144.